Twenty to Make

Pewter
Jewellery

Sandy Griffiths

Search Press

First published in 2014

Search Press Limited
Wellwood, North Farm Road,
Tunbridge Wells, Kent TN2 3DR

Text copyright © Sandy Griffiths 2014

Photographs by Ivan Naudé

Copyright © Search Press Ltd 2014

Print ISBN: 978-1-78221-080-1
Epub ISBN: 978-1-78126-229-0
Mobi ISBN: 978-1-78126-230-6

Suppliers
If you have difficulty in obtaining any of the
materials and equipment mentioned in this
book, then please visit the Search Press website
for details of suppliers: www.searchpress.com

Printed in China

Dedication
*To Audrey Griffiths, my wingman, and
Donna & Andrew Ingram, my quiet support.*

Acknowledgements
Please raise your glasses to Metz Press
whose stable I have been part of since 2006.
Ivan Naudé the very talented photographer
who makes magic with my work, and to
all my students and fellow pewterers
who inspire and encourage me,
especially Noelene Palmer-Rattray.

Contents

Introduction

This book is all about pewter art, and how to use it to create beautiful pieces of jewellery. Pewter art is accomplished by creating designs on sheets of pewter, using special tools. This is completely different from cast pewter, which involves melting down the pewter and pouring it into moulds to make items such as wine goblets, bowls, serving spoons, and so on. Pewter sheets are soft and pliable, so they will bend easily and can be transformed into wonderful creations. Because pewter sheets are flexible, they are used for decorative purposes, but they do need to be adhered to a supportive background.

Pewter jewellery

Using sheets of pewter to make jewellery is versatile, exiting and rewarding. You can make your own beautiful, antique-style bracelets and earrings, or contemporary brooches and stylish pendants. It's a great way to revamp the old or restyle the new, as well as to shake out the imagination while working out how to create a splendid piece.

Some items are completely covered with pewter to provide a solid silver look and to allow the pewter design to stand proud; some have just a suggestion of pewter to enhance an already attractive design. Add colour and texture by using semi-precious stones, flat-back crystals and rhinestones, coloured beads and felt, glass paints, metal foils and leather.

When you are looking for bracelets to cover, bear in mind that those cheap, plastic bracelets work fabulously, but make sure they are not too bevelled. Covering a sphere or a very rounded area with pewter will cause the pewter to gather and crease. The face of what you are covering with pewter should be quite flat. Bear this in mind, too, when you are looking for beads and earrings to spruce up. I made use of polymer clay to create supportive bases for my brooches.

There are 20 projects to choose from, so why wait any longer - pick the one you want to make and let's go!

Tools and Materials

Basic pewter kit

Tracer tool – A small ball tip or rounded tip similar to a knitting needle; used for 'drawing' the design on to the face of the pewter.

Cardboard – The cardboard from the back of the tracing paper pad will work well.

Thick tracing paper (90 gsm) and **HB pencil**

Masking tape

Glue – Any glue compatible with both metal and the surface on to which you are affixing it. I use silicon-based glue for the pewter, and clear epoxy glue to adhere crystals, beads and semi-precious stones to the pewter design.

You will also need

Medium ball-tool – Used to create thick, raised lines.

Paper pencil (or torchon) – Used to flatten and neaten the area on each side of the raised lines.

Piece of **felt** approximately A4 size

Craft knife, **steel ruler** and self-healing **cutting mat**

Needle-point cutter

Circle template (stencil of various sized circles)

Oval template (stencil of various sized ovals)

Small, **pointy pair of scissors** and a pair of **curved nail scissors**

Wax stick – Used to pick up and place flat-back crystals on to the pewter design. Make this by dipping the point of a kebab stick into hot wax, and then allowing it to cool.

Clear spray varnish – Pewter often blackens a little in time. To prevent this, spray a thin coat of clear varnish over the finished article to protect it. This is optional. If you are going to do this, it must be done after the polishing process, but before adding jewels, stones or paint.

Techniques

Low relief and high relief

Two techniques are used when doing pewter work: low relief and high relief. Low relief can be done from the front or the back of the pewter. If done from the front, the design will be indented and, therefore, hold more patina and polish, so the design lines will become black. If done from the back of the pewter, the design lines will be slightly raised (but are not high relief), they will not hold the patina and polish, and hence will be shiny. The design does not have to be filled with beeswax as it is not high enough. We can create lovely, fine designs using this technique.

For high relief we model out the design from the back of the pewter in order to create the raised image on the front. The indentations in the back are then filled with beeswax or crack filler to support the design and prevent it from being pressed flat.

All the projects in this book are done in low relief.

Polishing process

This is the final – and most rewarding – step. This process will add depth to the design as the patina and polish sit darkest in the indented areas of the design.

Polishing materials:

Hard, non-textured surface

Cotton wool

Rubber or latex gloves

Tissues

Turpentine

Baby powder

Patina

Household metal polish

Instructions:

1 Place the pewter with its design side up on to the hard surface. Clean the front of the pewter, first with a piece of cotton wool dipped into turpentine, then with a clean piece of cotton wool dipped into the baby powder. Note: the patina will not take if the pewter is not clean.

2 Wearing the gloves, absorb a little patina on to a small piece of cotton wool and apply evenly over the piece of pewter. It will blacken very quickly; once black, stop applying patina.

3 Rinse the pewter under the tap and pat dry with a tissue.

4 Absorb a little metal polish on to a piece of cotton wool and rub it over the face of the pewter. Buff off gently with a clean piece of cotton wool.

Caution: Rubbing too hard or buffing dry polish will remove the top layer of the pewter, making it duller.

Charm Bracelet

Materials:

Silver chain suitable for a charm bracelet

6 pearl beads

6 headpins

9 jump rings

Bolt ring clasp

Resin and hardener

Tools:

Pewter and basic pewter kit (page 6)

Polishing materials (page 7)

Circle template

Needle-point cutter

Self-healing cutting mat

Piece of felt

Paper cup and wooden lollypop stick

Toothpick

2 pairs of flat-nose pliers

Round-nose pliers

Side cutters

Instructions:

1 Trace a design of your choice (see page 48) on to the tracing paper using the HB pencil.

2 Place the pewter on to the cardboard and secure with two pieces of masking tape. Using the circle template and the tracer tool, trace two circles each measuring 2cm (¾in) in diameter on to the pewter. Then trace two more circles, one size smaller.

3 Place the tracing paper containing the traced design over one of the larger circles, making sure it is centred. Secure it with tape.

4 Using the tracer tool, trace the design on to the pewter. Remove the tracing paper and masking tape. Trace the design on to the second large circle.

5 Complete the polishing process.

6 Place the pewter, right side up, on to the self-healing cutting mat and secure well with tape. Place the 2cm (¾in) circle of the circle template over one of the 2cm (¾in) circles on the pewter. Hold down firmly. Run the needle-point cutter around the template to cut out the circle. You may need to run the cutter around a number of times. You can use a pair of nail scissors instead, but using the needle-point cutter will ensure a more precise circle.

7 Cut out all four circles.

8 To make up one charm, you will need two larger circles containing the design and two small, plain circles. Glue the two small circles of pewter together. Spread glue on to the reverse side of the circles that contain the design, sandwich the small circles between the two larger circles, and press together firmly. Wipe away any excess glue. The circle of pewter sandwiched in the centre will strengthen the charm.

9 Fold the piece of felt in half and place it on to the self-healing cutting mat. Place the charm on to the felt and make a hole in the top of the circle by pushing the needle-point cutter through the pewter.

10 Repeat Steps 1 to 9 to complete the other six charms.

11 Mix resin according to the manufacturer's instructions. Apply a thin layer of resin to one side of each charm. Leave to set for at least 24 to 48 hours. Use the toothpick to clear any resin from the hole before the resin has set. Once the resin has set mix more resin and hardener, and coat the other side of the charms. Leave to set and use the toothpick to clear any resin from the hole before the resin has set, as before.

12 Use the flat-nose pliers to open a jump ring, hook a pewter charm on to the jump ring, and then hook it on to the chain. Close the jump ring using the pliers. Repeat to attach all seven charms evenly spaced.

13 Thread the pearls on to the headpins and use the pliers to make loops to attach the pearl beads to the chain. Place a pearl after each charm.

14 Using the pliers and two jump rings, attach the lobster clasp and bolt ring to the bracelet.

Dragonfly Cuff Bracelet

Materials:

Pewter (enough for the outside and the inside of the bracelet)

Inexpensive metal cuff bracelet

Clear flat-back crystals

Tools:

Basic pewter kit (page 6)

Polishing materials (page 7)

Medium ball-tool

Paper pencil

Piece of felt

Wax stick and kebab stick

Small scissors

Instructions:

1 To transfer the shape of the bracelet on to the tracing paper, cut a strip of tracing paper slightly larger than the width and length of the bracelet. Wrap the tracing paper over the face of the bracelet, from end to end. Secure each end to the bracelet with masking tape.

2 Fold the excess tracing paper over the edges of the bracelet to create a crease line. Remove the tracing paper from the bracelet and remove the masking tape; flatten out the tracing paper. You now have the shape of the bracelet on the tracing paper in the form of a crease line. Draw over the crease line with the HB pencil.

3 Trace the dragonfly design on page 48 on to this piece of tracing paper. Remember to centre the design.

4 Place the pewter on to the cardboard and secure it with masking tape. Position the tracing paper on to the pewter and secure it with tape. Use the tracer tool to trace the shape of the bracelet on to the pewter. Don't press hard; a faint line will suffice. Remove the tracing paper and masking tape. Be careful not to tear the tracing paper.

5 Turn over the pewter and place it on to the piece of felt. Secure it with tape. Position the tracing paper on to the pewter, making sure the dragonfly design fits the bracelet shape that was traced on to the pewter.

6 Use the medium ball-tool to trace the dragonfly. Trace everything except the tiny veins on the inside of the wings. Remove the tracing paper and tape.

7 Turn over the pewter and place it on to the cardboard. Use the paper pencil to 'draw' on each side of the raised design lines to flatten those areas and to define the raised design lines. Repeat this step a second time, but use the tracer tool instead of the paper pencil.

8 Trace the veins on to the inside of the wings, using the tracer tool. You can either do this freehand, or by replacing the tracing paper and tracing the veins.

9 Complete a fine scribble pattern on the background of the pewter design. A textured pattern is a good idea on high traffic items as it will prevent scratches from showing.

10 Complete the polishing process. Use the pair of scissors to cut away the excess pewter; leave about 3mm (⅛in) of pewter outside the bracelet line. The strip of pewter needs to be slightly larger than the bracelet as we need to have enough pewter to fold over the edge of the bracelet.

11 Cut a strip of pewter to fit the inside of the cuff bracelet, with a 3mm (⅛in) overlap, polish it and then glue it into position. Fold the overlap of pewter over the edge of the bracelet and run the side of the tracer tool along the edge to mould the pewter around the bracelet's edge. Repeat this step for the pewter strip that lines the outside of the bracelet. When applying the glue make sure that the indentations of the dragonfly are filled with glue. I would suggest giving the back and front of the pewter bracelet a light spray with clear varnish (see Tools and Techniques, page 6-7).

12 Dip the kebab stick into the glue and place a small dab of glue on to the pewter where the crystals will be placed. Pick up the individual crystals with the tip of the wax stick and place each crystal on to the glue. Allow the glue to dry thoroughly.

Gemstone Cuff Bracelet

Trace the outline of your flat-back gem stones to determine the size of the oval. Glue the gemstones on to the bracelet only once you have covered the bracelet with the pewter.

Black Feather Bracelet

Materials:

Thin beading elastic

Small black beads

2 black, multi-hole spacers (about 10 holes)

Pewter

Tools:

Basic pewter kit (page 6)

Polishing materials (page 7)

Medium ball-tool

Paper pencil

Piece of felt

Craft knife and metal ruler

Self-healing cutting mat

Nail scissors

Instructions:

1 Place the multi-hole spacer on to the tracing paper and trace the edges with the HB pencil. Centre the feather design in the pencilled spacer shape on the tracing paper and trace it using the HB pencil.

2 Place the pewter on to the cardboard and secure in place with two pieces of masking tape. Position the tracing paper on to the pewter and secure it with tape. Trace the rectangle on to the pewter, using the tracer tool. Do not press hard.

3 Carefully remove the masking tape and tracing paper without tearing the paper. Turn over the pewter, place it on to the piece of felt and secure it with tape. Place the tracing paper on to the pewter, lining it up with the traced rectangle on the pewter. Using the medium ball-tool, trace the stem of the feather on to the pewter. Press firmly.

4 Remove all masking tape and tracing paper. Turn over the pewter, raised line facing you, and place it on to the cardboard.

5 Use the paper pencil to 'draw' on each side of the raised design line to flatten those areas and to define the raised design line. Repeat this

step a second time, but instead of using the paper pencil, use the tracer tool.

6 Use the tracer tool to create the quills of the feather. I prefer to do this freehand, but you can trace them from the tracing paper if you find this easier. Press firmly with the tracer tool when drawing the quills.

7 Using the same process, create another pewter feather design for the second spacer bead and complete the polishing process.

8 Place the pewter on to the cutting mat, and use the metal ruler and the craft cutter to cut along the lines of the rectangles. Use the pair of nail scissors to trim the corners of the rectangle ever so slightly. This prevents pointy corners that catch on clothing.

9 Make up the beaded bracelet using the small black beads, the multi-hole spacers and the beading elastic.

10 Spread glue on to the back of the pewter designs, making sure the indentation of the feather stem is filled with glue. Stick the designs on to the faces of the spacers. Once the designs are in place, run the edge of the tracer tool along the edges of the spacers to flatten the edges. Allow the glue to dry.

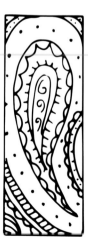

Pink Paisley Bracelet

Trace the paisley design on to the front of the pewter using the tracer tool. Once the pewter design has been glued on to the multi-hole spacer, decorate it with flat-back crystals. I used star- and teardrop-shaped crystals.

Leather & Pewter Bracelet

Materials:

Strip of leather, 3cm (1¼in) x 17cm (6¾in)

Pewter and basic pewter kit (page 6)

2 D-rings

Silver chain, about 5cm (2in)

4 silver jump rings

Silver toggle clasp

Tools:

2 pairs of flat-nose pliers

Side cutters

Circle template

Steel ruler and craft knife

Self-healing cutting mat

Nail scissors

Needle-point cutter

2 clothes pegs

Instructions:

1 Trace the circular design on to the tracing paper using the HB pencil. Use the circle template to trace the circles. The outside circle measures 2.7cm (1in) in diameter.

2 Place the pewter on to the cardboard; secure it with two pieces of masking tape.

3 Place the traced design on to the pewter and use the tracer tool to trace the design on to the pewter. Remember to use the circle template when tracing the circles. Press firmly.

4 Remove the tracing paper and masking tape. Use the tracer tool to complete a fine scribble pattern on the background of the pewter design.

5 Using the tracer tool and ruler, 'draw' two rectangles on to the pewter, each one measuring 8mm (⅓in) by 60mm (2½in). Complete a fine scribble pattern on each rectangle using the tracer tool.

6 Complete the polishing process.

7 Cut out the rectangles using the steel ruler, craft knife and cutting mat. Cut out the circle, using the nail scissors. Tape the circular pewter design on to the cutting mat and use the needle-point cutter to cut out the small square in the centre of the design.

8 Glue the circular pewter design on to the centre of the leather bracelet. Glue the pewter strips to each side of the pewter circle, leaving a gap of 15mm (⅔in); fold the pewter strips to the back of the leather bracelet. Press down firmly. Allow the glue to dry.

9 Using the nail scissors, round all corners of the leather strip.

10 Place one end of the leather strip through the D-ring, fold it over and glue it in place. The fold-over should be about 20mm (¾in). Repeat this for the other end of the bracelet. Secure each fold with a clothes peg until the glue has dried.

11 Cut the silver chain in half, using the side cutters. Use flat-nose pliers to open a jump ring and then, holding the jump ring with one pair of pliers, hook the D-ring and one length of silver chain on to it. Close the loop of the jump ring with the second pair of pliers.

12 Use the pliers to open a second jump ring, hook the end of the chain and the toggle bar on to the jump ring, then close the loop with the second pair of pliers.

13 Repeat this process to attach the chain and toggle ring to the other end of the leather bracelet.

Chunky Pewter Bracelet

Materials:

Inexpensive plastic bracelet

Tools:

Pewter and basic pewter kit (page 6)

Polishing materials (page 7)

Scissors

Instructions:

1 Measure the circumference of the bracelet and then the width, adding 4mm (⅛in) to the width (but not the circumference) measurement to allow an overlap. Cut a tracing paper pattern to fit these measurements.

2 Place the bracelet on to a piece of tracing paper and trace the outer and inner circumference of the bracelet; cut out to create a circular paper pattern.

3 Cut out the pewter to size, using these paper patterns as guides. You will need two strips of pewter, one for the inside and the other for the outside of the bracelet. You will also have to cut out two circles, one for each side of the bracelet.

4 Trace the design for the face of the bracelet (see page 48) on to the long paper pattern.

5 Place the long strip of pewter on to the cardboard and secure with masking tape. Place the traced design on to the pewter; secure with tape. Using the tracer tool, trace the design on to the pewter. Press firmly.

6 Trace the circle design on to the circular paper pattern. Place a circle of pewter on to the cardboard, and secure it with tape; then position the traced design on the pewter and secure with masking tape. Using the tracer tool, trace the pattern on to the pewter. Repeat this process for the second circle of pewter.

7 Complete the polishing process for all four pieces of pewter.

8 Glue the strip of pewter that lines the inside of the bracelet into position. Fold the overlap of pewter over the edge of the bracelet and run the side of the tracer tool along the edge to mould the pewter around the bracelet's edge. Repeat this step for the pewter strip that lines the outside of the bracelet. Ensure that the join on the outer strip is aligned with the join on the inner strip.

9 Glue a pewter circle to one side of the bracelet and press down well. Run the edge of the tracer tool along the inner and outer edges of the pewter to smooth and flatten them. Repeat these steps for the remaining circle on the other side.

10 To hide the pewter join, create a mock clasp by cutting a 5mm (⅛in) wide strip of pewter that is long enough to fit around the bracelet like a clasp. Polish the strip before gluing it into position.

Crystal Bracelet

Cover the bracelet with the pewter containing the low-relief design. Gently press the tip of the tracer tool into the pewter where the crystals will be placed to create an indentation. Place a tiny dot of glue into the indentation and place a crystal on to the glue in each indentation using a wax stick.

Felt Daisy Brooch

Materials:

Felt

Polymer clay

Brooch pin

Cotton

Flat-back crystals

Tools:

Pewter and basic pewter kit (page 6)

Polishing materials (page 7)

Circle template

Nail scissors

Scissors

Sewing needle and thread

Wax stick and kebab stick

Instructions:

1 Roll out a piece of polymer clay to approximately 2mm (⅛in) thick. Cut out a circle and bake according to the manufacturer's instructions.

2 Cut a circle of pewter large enough to cover the face and sides of the clay circle. Use the circle template and tracer tool to 'draw' a circle of the correct size on to the pewter, then cut out the circle using the nail scissors.

3 Trace the butterfly design on to the tracing paper using the HB pencil.

4 Place the pewter circle on to a piece of cardboard. Using two small pieces of masking tape, tape the pewter to the cardboard. Place the traced design on to the pewter. Remember to centre it and tape into position.

5 Using the tracer tool, trace over the pencil design. Press firmly.

6 Remove all the masking tape and tracing paper. If your design lines are not deep enough, retrace them using the tracer tool.

7 Complete the polishing process.

8 Apply glue to the back of the pewter design and stick it on to the polymer clay disc. Carefully fold the pewter over the sides of the disc. Once the pewter has been fixed, run the edge of the tracer tool around the edge of the disc to flatten the edges.

9 Cut out two large whorls of felt petals and one small felt whorl. Sew through the centre of the whorls to stitch them together.

10 Glue the pewter design on to the felt flower. Once the glue has dried, stitch the brooch pin to the back of the flower.

11 Dip the kebab stick into the glue and place a small dab of glue on to the pewter where the crystals will be positioned. Pick up the individual crystals with the tip of the wax stick and place each crystal on to the glue.

Blue Felt Rose Brooch

Cut irregularly shaped circles of blue felt and cut green felt leaves; stitch these together to create a rose. Complete the pewter centre by following the method used for the daisy brooch, and using the rose template.

Web Brooch

Materials:

3 pieces of pewter

Blue glass paint (solvent-based)

Glass paint solvent, in a small glass bowl

Small, clear, flat-back crystals

Resin and hardener

Brooch pin

Tools:

Basic pewter kit (page 6)

Polishing materials (page 7)

Medium ball-tool

Paper pencil

Piece of felt

Needle-point cutter and self-healing cutting mat

Soft, pointy watercolour paintbrush

Wax stick and kebab stick

Instructions:

1 Trace the design on to tracing paper using the HB pencil.

2 Place the pewter on to the felt; secure it in place with two pieces of tape. Place the traced design on to the pewter and secure it with tape.

3 Trace the web using the medium ball-tool. Remove the tracing paper and masking tape.

4 Turn the pewter over, and place it on to the cardboard. Use the paper pencil to 'draw' on each side of the raised design lines to flatten those areas and to define the raised design lines. Repeat this step a second time, but use the tracer tool instead of the paper pencil.

5 Complete the polishing process.

6 Place the pewter spider web on to the self-healing cutting mat. Cut out the web using the needle-point cutter.

7 Apply glue to the back of the web, making sure that you fill the indentations, then stick it on to a second piece of pewter. Allow it to dry.

8 Place the web on to the self-healing cutting mat and cut it out carefully, using the needle-point cutter.

9 Glue the pewter web to the third piece of pewter, allow the glue to dry, and then cut out the web using the needle-point cutter. The three layers of pewter will strengthen the brooch.

10 For added strength, apply a layer of resin to the back of the brooch. Mix the resin and hardener according to manufacturer's instructions.

11 When the resin has set, which may take 24 to 48 hours, fill the background of the web with blue glass paint. Dip the paintbrush into the blue glass paint and allow the paint to flow between the raised lines of the web. If you accidently get paint on the raised area, it can be removed as follows: Dip a clean brush into the solvent; remove excess solvent by dabbing the brush against the side of the bowl; then brush the tip of the paintbrush over the unwanted paint. Allow the paint to dry overnight.

12 Use the tip of the tracer tool to make tiny indentations on the raised web where the crystals will be placed. These indentations will hold the glue.

13 Dip the kebab stick into the glue and place a small dab of glue on to the pewter where the crystals will be placed. Pick up the individual crystals with the tip of the wax stick and place each crystal on to the glue. Allow the glue to dry thoroughly.

14 Glue the brooch pin on to the back of the brooch.

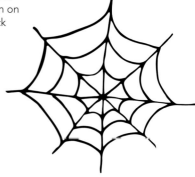

20

Leather Brooch

Materials:

Pewter

Polymer clay

Brown leather

Flat-back, semi-precious stone

Brooch pin

Brown acrylic paint

Tools:

Basic pewter kit (page 6)

Polishing materials (page 7)

Piece of felt

Medium ball-tool

Paper pencil

Oval template

Small, pointy pair of scissors

Instructions:

1 Trace the design on to the tracing paper using the HB pencil.

2 Place the pewter on to the piece of felt and secure it with masking tape.

3 Place the oval template on to the pewter and then, using the medium ball-tool, trace an oval on to the pewter. The length of the oval should be about 55mm (2¼in).

4 Remove the stencil and masking tape. Turn over the pewter and place it on to the cardboard. Use the paper pencil to 'draw' on each side of the raised design lines to flatten

those areas and to define the raised design line. Repeat this step a second time, but use the tracer tool instead of the paper pencil.

5 Place the pewter on to the cardboard; the raised line of the oval should be facing you. Place the traced design on to the pewter and tape into position. Use the tracer tool to trace the design on to the pewter. Press firmly.

6 Remove the tracing paper and tape.

7 Complete the polishing process. Cut out the pewter design using the pair of scissors.

8 Use the oval template to draw an oval on to the back of the leather. It should be about 5mm (¼in) larger than the pewter design. Cut it out.

9 Apply glue to the back of the pewter, making sure the indentation of the oval is filled with glue. Stick the pewter design in place on the leather oval. Allow the glue to dry.

10 Roll out a piece of polymer clay, about 2mm (⅛in) thick. Cut out an oval that is the same size as the leather oval. Bake the clay in the oven according to manufacturer's instructions.

11 Paint the clay oval brown.

12 Glue the leather and pewter design to the painted clay. Glue the semi-precious stone in place on the pewter. Allow the glue to dry.

13 Glue the brooch pin to the back of the brooch.

Painted Brooch

Using a small, soft, pointy watercolour bush, paint clear solvent-based glass paint on to the face of the pewter, inside the raised oval. While the clear paint is still wet, apply a little purple glass paint to one half of the design and blue to the other half. Use a clean brush to work the colours into the clear paint.

Crystal & Pewter Earrings

Materials:

Pewter

Pair of ear wires

Pair of eye pins

2 round crystal beads

2 square crystal beads

6 small silver beads

4 tiny, flat-back, clear crystals

Resin and hardener

Tools:

Basic pewter kit (page 6)

Polishing materials (page 7)

Circle template

Needle-point cutter

Self-healing cutting mat

Piece of felt

Paper cup and wooden lollypop stick

Toothpick

2 pairs of flat-nose pliers

Round-nose pliers

Side cutters

Wax stick and kebab stick

Instructions:

1 Trace the web design on page 48 on to tracing paper using the HB pencil.

2 Place the pewter on to the cardboard, and secure it in place with masking tape. Using the circle template and the tracer tool, trace four circles each measuring about 2cm (¾in) in diameter. Then trace two more circles, one size smaller.

3 Place the tracing paper containing the web design over one of the larger circles, making sure it is centred; secure it with tape.

4 Using the tracer tool, trace the design on to the pewter. Remove the tracing paper and masking tape. Trace the web design on to the other three large circles.

5 Complete the polishing process.

6 Place the pewter, right side up, on to the self-healing cutting mat and secure it well with tape. Place the 2cm (¾in) circle of the circle template over one of the 2cm (¾in) circles on the pewter, and press down firmly. Run the needle-point cutter around the template to cut out the circle. You may need to run the cutter around the circle a number of times. You can use a pair of nail scissors instead, but using the needle-point cutter will ensure a more precise circle.

7 Cut out all the circles.

8 To make up one earring, you need two larger circles containing the web design, and one small, plain circle. Apply glue to the reverse side of each circle that contains the design, sandwich the small circle between the two larger circles, and press together firmly. Wipe away any excess glue. The circle of pewter sandwiched in the centre will strengthen the earring. Repeat this process for the second earring.

9 Fold the piece of felt in half and place it on to the self-healing cutting mat. Place one of the earrings on to the felt and make a hole in the top of the circle by pushing the needle-point cutter through the pewter. Repeat this for the second earring.

10 Mix resin according to the manufacturer's instructions. Apply a thin layer of resin to one side of each earring and allow to set for 24-48 hours. Use the toothpick to clear any resin from the hole before it has set. Once the resin has set, repeat on the other side of the earrings.

11 Use the flat-nose pliers to open the loop of the eye pin, then hook the pewter design on to the loop and close the loop on the eye pin with the pliers.

12 Thread the beads onto the eye pin. Use the flat-nose pliers and the round-nose pliers to create a loop at the top of the eye pin. Before closing the loop slip the ear wire into the loop.

13 Use the kebab stick to place a dot of glue onto the centre of the web, pick up a crystal with the wax stick, and position it on the dot of glue. Place a crystal on the back and front of both pewter webs.

Pearl & Pewter Earrings

Materials:

Pewter

Pair of ear wires

Pair of headpins

2 large, ball-shaped beads (pearl colour)

2 disc-shaped beads

2 pewter-coloured beads

2 small silver beads

4 flat-back pearls

Tools:

Basic pewter kit (page 6)

Polishing materials (page 7)

2 pairs of flat-nose pliers

Round-nose pliers

Side cutters

Small ball and cup tool

Piece of felt

Medium ball-tool

Paper pencil

Circle template

Nail scissors

Instructions:

1 Place the pewter on to the cardboard and secure with masking tape. Using the circle template and tracer tool, draw four circles on to the pewter. They must be large enough to cover the face of the disc-shaped beads. You will need four circles as you need to cover the front and back of the beads, because the beads will swivel when they are worn.

2 Place the pewter on to the piece of felt and secure it with masking tape. Using the medium ball-tool and circle template, 'draw' a circle in the centre of each pewter circle. The circle must be slightly larger than the flat-back pearl, so that the pearl will fit snugly into the raised circle of pewter.

3 Remove the template and masking tape. Turn over the pewter and place it on to the cardboard. Use the paper pencil to 'draw' on each side of the raised design lines to flatten those areas and to define the raised design lines. Repeat this step a second time, but use the tracer tool instead of the paper pencil.

4 Place the pewter on to the cardboard with the raised circle facing you; complete the rest of the design. Use the circle template and tracer tool to 'draw' the circles; complete grooves along the border and the scribble pattern around the raised circle with the tracer tool.

5 To create the circle of raised dots, place the pewter on to the felt, its wrong side facing up. Using the ball end of the ball and cup tool, press a circle of indentations into the pewter; then turn over the pewter, its right side now facing up, place it on to the cardboard and press the 'cup' over the raised bumps to neaten them. If you don't have a ball and cup tool, you can create the raised dots by 'drawing' a small circle on the face of the pewter using the tracer tool and a circle template. Turn over the pewter, place it on to the felt and press out the dot using the tip of the paper pencil. Place the pewter with its right side up on to the cardboard and define the raised dot by first using the paper pencil and then the tracer tool.

6 Complete the polishing process and then cut out the four circles using the pair of nail scissors.

7 Glue a circle of pewter on to the back and front of each disc-shaped bead. Once the pewter is in place, run the edge of the tracer tool around the edge of the disc to flatten the edges. Glue the flat-back pearls in place. Allow the glue to dry.

8 Thread the beads on to the headpin and make a 90 degree bend just above the top bead, using the flat-nose pliers. Use the side cutters to cut the wire, leaving a tail of about 8mm (⅓in) long. Position the round-nose pliers at the tip of the tail, making sure the tail faces away from your body. Wrap the wire towards you to create a loop. Before closing the loop, slip the ear wire on to the loop, and continue wrapping the wire towards you to close.

Purple Earrings

Using the tracer tool, 'draw' four circles and four squares on to a piece of pewter. Complete a low relief design of your choice on each shape. Polish, cut out and glue the design on to the purple beads. Make up your earrings or look for a similar pair of ready-made earrings to adorn with pewter.

Swan Earrings

Materials:

Pair of ear wires

Pair of inexpensive earrings, shape similar to
that used here

Pewter

4 tear-shaped, flat-back crystals

Tools:

Basic pewter kit (page 6)

Polishing materials (page 7)

2 pairs of flat-nosed pliers

Wax stick and kebab stick

Needle-point cutter

Self-healing cutting mat

Nail scissors

Instructions:

1 Remove the ear wires from the earrings.
Transfer the shape of the earrings on to the
tracing paper by placing the earrings on to the
tracing paper and tracing the outlines with the
HB pencil.

2 Trace the swan design on to the tracing
paper. If necessary, alter the design to fit the
shape of your earrings.

3 Place the pewter on to the cardboard, and
trace four earring shapes on to the pewter,
using the tracer tool; two to cover the front of
the earrings, and two to cover the back.

4 Place the pewter on to the cardboard; secure
it with masking tape. Line up the traced design
with one of the earring shapes on the pewter;
secure with tape.

5 Using the tracer tool and pressing firmly,
trace over the pencil design.

6 Remove the masking tape and tracing paper.
If your design lines are not deep enough,
retrace them, using the tracer tool.

7 Use the tracer tool to do a fine scribble
pattern over the areas between the designs;

you will still be working on the cardboard.

8 Complete the second earring following the
same steps.

9 Polish the four earring shapes.

10 Cut out the oval holes in all four of the
earring shapes, using the needle-point cutter
and self-healing cutting mat.

11 Using the nail scissors, cut out the four
earring shapes about 1mm (⅛in) larger than
the actual traced earring shape, so that there
is enough pewter to cover the sides of the
earrings.

12 Apply glue to the back of the pewter
designs and stick them on to the face of the
earrings. Carefully fold the pewter over the
sides of the earrings. Once the pewter is in
place, run the edge of the tracer tool around
the edge of the disc to flatten the edges.

13 Repeat this process to stick the plain
pewter pieces to the back of the earrings.
Allow the glue to dry.

14 Dip the kebab stick into the glue and place
a small dab of glue on to the pewter where the
crystals will be placed. Pick up the individual
crystals with the tip of the wax stick and place
each crystal on to the glue. Allow the glue to
dry thoroughly.

15 Use the flat-nose pliers to attach the
earrings to the ear wires by opening and
closing the loops on the ear wires.

Butterfly Necklace

Materials:

20 flat, round, green beads

Small silver beads

Clear beading thread

2 crimp beads

Toggle clasp with rose detail

Pewter

Tools:

Basic pewter kit (page 6)

Polishing materials (page 7)

Glue

Tissues

Flat-nose pliers

Paper craft punch – butterfly shape

Scissors

Instructions:

1 Punch out 20 butterflies from the pewter. This is a good time to use small scraps of pewter. You do not need to polish the pewter first.

2 Glue the butterflies on to ten beads. Glue a butterfly on to both sides of each bead, because the beads will swivel while you are wearing them. Check the position of the butterflies on your beads. I have placed all my butterflies in the same direction; their winged sides line up with the holes through the bead.

3 Cut a strand of beading thread that is about 12cm (¾in) longer than the required length of the necklace. This will leave a comfortable length for attaching the clasps. Slide a crimp bead on to one end of the beading thread.

Add the bar of the toggle clasp, loop the beading thread back through the crimp bead and draw it up against the clasp. Using the flat-nose pliers, flatten the crimp bead into place. Make sure the crimp bead is secured well and that it does not slide along the thread.

4 String all of the beads on to the beading thread; the first few beads should be threaded on to both thicknesses of the thread. Separate the flat, green beads using the small, silver beads. Every alternate green bead will have a pewter butterfly on it.

5 Slide the second crimp bead on to the beading thread. Pass the thread through the other end of the toggle clasp and then back through the crimp as well as several other beads. Pull the thread until all of the beads lie snugly against each other, and then flatten the crimp bead with the pliers. Cut off the excess beading thread with a pair of scissors.

Black and Silver Necklace

You will need long strips of pewter, about 5mm (¼in) wide. It is easier to work with two or three long pieces, which you then cut to size to fit each bead, than to work with twenty small strips. Create a continuous pattern on the pewter using the tracer tool. Patina and polish the pewter strips; then cut them to size and glue them on to the beads. This must be done on both sides of each bead. Adorn the pewter with flat-back crystals.

Funky Heart Necklace

Materials:

Pink, square beads and pink seed beads

Wooden heart painted pink

Beading thread for stringing beads

Pink, flat-back crystals

Small eye hook

Jump ring

Pewter

Tools:

Basic pewter kit (page 6)

Polishing materials (page 7)

2 pairs of flat-nosed pliers

Small scissors

Wax stick and kebab stick

Instructions:

1 Make up the beaded necklace by threading the beads on to the beading thread, alternating one seed bead and one square bead. A suitable, ready-made necklace is also an option.

2 Trace the heart design on to the tracing paper using the HB pencil. Place the pewter on to the cardboard; secure it in place with masking tape. Place the traced design on to the pewter and secure it with tape.

3 Trace the design on to the pewter using the tracer tool.

4 Complete the polishing process.

5 Cut out the heart design, using the small pair of scissors, and glue it in place on to the pink wooden heart.

6 Screw the small eye hook into the top of the wooden heart.

7 Use the flat-nose pliers to open the jump ring, hook the eye hook and necklace on to the jump ring, and then close the jump ring using the pliers.

8 Dip the kebab stick into the glue and place a small dab of glue on to the pewter where the crystals will be placed. Pick up the individual crystals with the tip of the wax stick and place each crystal on to the glue. Allow the glue to dry thoroughly.

Bird Heart

Complete the bird and sun using the same techniques used for the pewter heart. Do a fine scribble pattern on the bird to create the velvety, feathered look. I have attached it to a necklace of African teething beads. The grey of the beads complements the colour of the pewter.

Materials:

7 rectangular wooden beads

8 oval wooden beads

1,5m (1⅔yd) brown silk ribbon
 (15mm (⅝in) wide)

Pewter

Tools:

Basic pewter kit (page 6)

Polishing materials (page 7)

Craft knife steel ruler

Self-healing cutting mat

Scissors

Instructions:

1 Trace the designs on to the tracing paper using the HB pencil. There are three designs; two are repeated. You will need to create 14 pewter designs, one for the front and back of each rectangular bead, because the beads will swivel while you are wearing them.

2 Place the pewter on to the cardboard and secure it with masking tape. Place the traced designs on to the pewter and secure them with tape. I find it easier to trace all the designs on to one piece of pewter, and then cut them out once I have polished the pewter. This way you polish only once, not 14 times. Make sure your designs are correctly spaced so that the pewter can be cut to the correct size. My pieces of pewter

measure 1.5cm (⅔in) x 4cm (1¾in) each. Adjust the size of yours according to the size of your rectangular beads.

3 Trace the designs on to the pewter, using the tracer tool. Press firmly.

4 Remove the tracing paper and masking tape.

5 Complete the polishing process.

6 Using the craft knife, cutting mat and steel ruler, cut each design to size.

7 Glue the pewter designs to the front and back of each rectangular bead. Allow the glue to dry thoroughly.

8 Thread the beads on to the ribbon; start and end with an oval bead. Tie a single knot between two consecutive beads. Tie the ends of the ribbon into a bow.

Turquoise Flower Necklace

Materials:

Bag of turquoise seed beads

Doughnut-shaped, semi-precious turquoise stone

Beading thread

20 crimp beads (approximately)

2 eye pins

Toggle clasp with leaf design

4 silver jump rings

2 silver cone beads

Pewter

Tools:

Basic pewter kit (page 6)

Polishing materials (page 7)

2 pairs of flat-nose pliers

Side cutters

Round-nose pliers

Scissors

Needle-point cutters and self-healing cutting mat

Circle template

Paper pencil

Instructions:

1 Trace the design on to the tracing paper using the HB pencil.

2 Place the pewter on to the cardboard and secure it with masking tape.

3 Position the tracing paper on to the pewter and secure it with tape. Using the tracer tool, trace the design on to the pewter; press firmly. Place the circle template on to the tracing paper, hold it down firmly, and use the tracer tool to trace a neat circle. Use a circle that corresponds with the size of the hole in your turquoise stone.

4 Remove the tracing paper and masking tape.

5 Complete the polishing process.

6 Place the pewter, right side up, on to the cutting mat and secure it with tape. Position the circle template over the circle on the pewter design. (You will use the same size circle as you did in Step 3.) Holding down the circle template firmly, run the point of the needle-point cutter around the circle to cut out a neat circle. You may need to run the point around two to three times.

7 Glue the pewter design into position on the stone. Run the tip of the paper pencil around the edges of the design to make sure they are stuck down well. Allow the glue to dry.

8 Make up a nine-strand necklace with the turquoise seed beads. Attach the toggle clasp with the leaf design to the necklace.

9 Cut two pieces of beading thread about 12cm (1¾in) long. Thread about 6cm (2⅓in) of turquoise seed beads onto each strand of beading thread. Take one strand of beads, thread the pewter adorned turquoise gemstone onto the strand, loop it around all ten strands of the necklace and secure it with a surgeon's knot. Repeat this with the second sting of beads.

Rose Quartz, Pewter and Crystals

Trace the design on to the pewter, and use the tracer tool to complete a fine scribble pattern on the square background. Adorn with pink, flat-backed crystals. Loop a fine silver chain through the centre.

Crazy Cat Pendant

Materials:

Silver chain

Rectangular photo pendant,
 4cm (2¾in) x 3cm (2¼in)

Resin and hardener

Pewter

Tools:

Basic pewter kit (page 6)

Polishing materials (page 7)

Paper cup and wooden lollypop stick

Craft knife and steel ruler

Self-healing cutting mat

Paper pencil

Instructions:

1 Trace the cat design on to the tracing paper using the HB pencil.

2 Place the pewter on to the cardboard. Secure it in place with masking tape. Position the traced design on to the pewter and secure it with masking tape.

3 Use the tracer tool to trace the design on to the pewter. Press firmly.

4 Complete the polishing process, and then cut out the pewter rectangle, using the craft knife, ruler and cutting mat.

5 Apply glue to the back of the pewter design. Place the pewter design into the photo pendant, pressing down firmly on the face of the pewter. Wipe away any excess glue with a tissue. Run the point of the paper pencil around the edges of the pewter design to mould the pewter into the inside edges of the pendant. Clean away any excess glue.

6 In the paper cup, mix a small amount of resin and hardener according to manufacturer's instructions. Apply the resin to the face of the pendant. The resin should be level with the sides; it must not flow over. Gently spread the resin over the pewter with the wooden lollypop stick, making sure the resin reaches the borders of the pendant. To remove air bubbles from the resin, exhale over the pendant. The warmth of your breath will cause the bubbles to rise to the surface. The pendant must lie flat while the resin is hardening, so place it on to the cardboard, making sure the chain holder at the top of the pendant is lying over the edge of the cardboard. To prevent dust from settling on the resin, you can place a box lid over the pendant. Most resins will need 24 to 48 hours to set.

7 Thread the silver chain through the top of the pendant.

Fish Pendant

Materials:

Copper-coloured tiger tail

Bolt ring clasp and jump ring (copper colour)

Pair of copper-coloured thong clamps

2 copper-coloured crimp tubes

Copper- and amber-coloured beads

Small, flat-back, amber-coloured crystal

Large round shell disc

Silver jump ring

Copper leaf paper

Wunda Size glue (for metal leaf papers)

Clear aerosol varnish

Piece of old stocking, about 15cm (3in) long

1 small ball of cotton wool

Pewter

Tools:

Basic pewter kit (page 6)

Polishing materials (page 7)

Soft, pointy watercolour paintbrush

Wax stick and kebab stick

2 pairs of flat-nose pliers

Nail scissors

Instructions:

1 Trace the design on to the tracing paper using the HB pencil.

2 Place the pewter on to the cardboard and secure it with masking tape. Place the shell disc on to the pewter and draw around it using the tracer tool. Do not press hard; a faint line will do.

3 Place the traced design on to the pewter; make sure it is positioned well in the circle. Secure it with tape.

4 Trace the fish design and the hearts on to the pewter, using the tracing tool. Press firmly. You may prefer to do the fine patterns on the fish freehand, without the tracing paper.

5 Remove tracing paper and masking tape.

6 Complete the polishing process.

7 Cut out the circle of pewter with the nail scissors. It must be about 1mm (⅛in) larger than the actual traced circle so that there is enough pewter to cover the sides of the shell disc. Apply glue to the back of the pewter design and place the design on to the face of the shell disc. Carefully fold the pewter over the sides of the pendant. Once the pewter is in place, run the edge of the tracer tool around the edges of the disc to flatten the pewter.

8 Paint a little Wunder Size glue on to each heart; allow the glue to dry completely; there must be no milky areas. Cut a strip of copper leaf and place it over the three hearts. Press down with the fingertips.

9 Make a sanding tool by placing the ball of cotton wool inside the strip of stocking. Tie the ends into a knot, and cut off the excess. Hold the sanding tool by the knot and rub the pad over the copper leaf to rub away the excess copper leaf paper. If there are any areas of copper leaf which stubbornly stick to the pewter outside the heart area, gently rub them away with a cotton bud dipped in turpentine.

10 Spray the pewter with clear varnish; this will protect the copper leaf paper and prevent further oxidisation of the pewter.

11 Dip the kebab stick into the glue and place a small dab of glue on to the fish's eye, where the crystal will be placed. Pick up the crystal with the tip of the wax stick and place on to the glue. Allow the glue to dry.

12 Make up the necklace by threading the beads on to a double strand of tiger tail and attach the clasp.

13 Using the flat-nosed pliers, open the silver jump ring and slide the pewter pendant on to it. Hook the jump ring in place on the necklace, and close the loop with the pliers.

Sunshine Pendant

Materials:

Silver link chain

Rectangular photo pendant
(4cm (1¾in) x 3cm (1¼in))

Glass paint (blue, orange, red and clear)

Glass paint solvent

Resin and hardener

Pewter

Tools:

Basic pewter kit (page 6)

Polishing materials (page 7)

Soft, pointy watercolour paintbrush

Piece of felt

Medium ball-tool

Paper pencil

Paper cup and wooden lollypop stick

Glass paint solvent in a small glass bowl

Craft knife and steel ruler

Self-healing cutting mat

Instructions:

1 Trace the sun design on to tracing paper using the HB pencil.

2 Place the pewter on to the piece of felt and secure it in place with tape.

3 Place the traced design on to the pewter and secure it in place with masking tape.

4 Trace the design on to the pewter, using the medium ball-tool.

5 Turn over the pewter and place it on to the cardboard. Use the paper pencil to 'draw' on each side of the raised design lines to flatten those areas and to define the raised design lines. Repeat this step a second time, but use the tracer tool instead of the paper pencil.

6 Complete the polishing process and then cut out the pewter rectangle, using the craft knife, ruler and cutting mat.

7 Spread glue on to the back of the pewter design, making sure the glue fills the indented areas. Place the pewter design into the photo pendant, pressing down firmly on the face of the pewter. Wipe away any excess glue with a tissue. Run the point of the paper pencil around the edges of the pewter design to mould the pewter into the inside edges of the pendant. Clean away any excess glue.

8 Dip the paintbrush into the clear glass paint and allow the paint to flow into the face area (not the eye and mouth) of the design. Using the paintbrush, work the clear paint toward the edges of the face area. Clean the brush in the solvent and wipe it dry with a tissue. Dip the paintbrush into the orange glass paint and paint over the clear paint on the face, using the paintbrush to mix the clear and orange paint. This must be done while the clear paint is still wet. Mixing the clear and orange paint creates a less intense orange colour. If you want a bold orange colour, use only the orange paint; do not apply the clear paint first.

9 Paint clear glass paint and then blue paint on to the eye area.

10 For the mouth, sun petals and sky, paint the colours directly on to the pewter without using the clear paint as a base coat. Always clean the brush in the solvent before changing colours. Leave the paint to dry overnight. If you need to clean paint off the pewter, dip the paintbrush into the solvent, dab the brush on the side of the bowl to get rid of excess solvent, and use the tip of the brush to wipe the area clean.

11 Mix resin according to manufacturer's instructions. Apply the resin to the face of the pendant. The resin should be level with the sides; it must not flow over. Most resins will need 24 to 48 hours to set.

12 Thread the silver chain through the top of the pendant.

Red Heart Pendant

I have used the same technique as the sun design to create the little heart. It is filled with red paint, and covered with resin. Create a stylish necklace using small, silver beads and red seed beads.

Yin and Yang Pendant

Materials:

Black thong

Pair of thong clamps

Lobster-claw clasp and jump ring

1 silver jump ring

Round photo pendant, 2,5cm (1in) diameter

Black glass paint

Glass paint solvent in a small glass bowl

Resin and hardener

Pewter

Tools:

Basic pewter kit (page 6)

Polishing materials (page 7)

Small, soft, pointy paintbrush

Piece of felt Medium ball-tool

Large ball and cup tool

Paper cup and wooden lollypop stick

Nail scissors

2 pairs of flat-nose pliers

Instructions:

1 Trace the yin–and–yang design on page 48 on to tracing paper using the HB pencil.

2 Place the pewter on to the piece of felt and secure it with tape.

3 Place the traced design on to the pewter and secure it with masking tape.

4 Trace the S-shape of the design on to the pewter using the medium ball-tool.

5 Turn over the pewter and place it on to cardboard. Use the paper pencil to 'draw' on each side of the raised design line to flatten those areas and to define the raised design line. Repeat this step a second time, but use the tracer tool instead of the paper pencil.

6 Use a large ball and cup tool to create the raised dots. Do this by placing the pewter, wrong side facing up, on to the piece of felt, so that the indentations of the S are facing

you. Press the ball firmly on to the pewter. Turn the pewter over, place it on to the cardboard and then press the cup end of the tool firmly over the raised dot. If you don't have a ball and cup tool, you can create the raised dots by 'drawing' a small circle on the face of the pewter, using the tracer tool and a circle template. Turn over the pewter, place it on to the felt and press out the dot using the tip of the paper pencil. Place the pewter, its right side facing up, on to the cardboard and define the area around the raised dot by first using the paper pencil, and then the tracer tool.

7 Complete the polishing process and then cut out the pewter circle using the pair of nail scissors.

8 Apply glue to the back of the pewter design, making sure the glue fills the indented areas. Place the pewter design into the photo pendant, pressing down firmly on the face of the pewter. Wipe away any excess glue with a tissue. Run the point of the paper pencil along the edges of the pewter design to mould the pewter into the inside edges of the pendant. Clean away any excess glue.

9 Dip the paintbrush into the black glass paint and allow the paint to flow into the required area, between the raised S and the edge of the pendant. If you need to clean paint off the pewter, dip the paintbrush into the solvent, dab the brush on the side of the bowl to get rid of excess solvent, and use the tip of the brush to wipe the area clean. Allow the paint to dry overnight.

10 Mix resin according to the manufacturer's instructions. Apply the resin to the face of the pendant. The resin should be level with the sides; it must not flow over. Allow to dry completely, usually 24 to 48 hours.

11 Thread the pendant onto the black thong; tie a knot on each side of the pendant.

12 Complete the necklace by attaching the lobster claw clasp using the pliers, the thong clamps and jump rings.

Jewellery Box

Materials:

Square wooden box

Piece of cork or felt for the underside
of the box

Pewter

Tools:

Basic pewter kit (page 6)

Polishing materials (page 7)

Craft knife and steel ruler

Self-healing cutting mat

Circle template

Pair of pointy scissors

Felt-tip marker

Instructions:

1 Using a photocopy machine, size the design on page 48 to fit the lid of your box. Trace the design on to the tracing paper using the HB pencil. Work accurately.

2 Cut the pewter to fit the lid. Place the pewter on to the piece of cardboard and secure it with masking tape. Position the traced design on to the pewter and secure it with tape.

3 Using the tracer tool, trace the design on to the pewter. Press firmly.

4 Remove the tracing paper and masking tape. With the pewter still on the cardboard, use the tracer tool to add your own desired details to the design. Use your imagination and just have fun. I have done a scribble background, which is optional. I generally do a scribble pattern on projects which will be high traffic items as it will hide marks and scratches.

5 Complete the polishing process.

6 Glue the pewter design on to the lid of the box. Once in place, run the edge of the tracer tool along the edges of the box lid to flatten the edges.

7 Cut the cork or felt to the exact size of the box and glue it to the underside of the box.

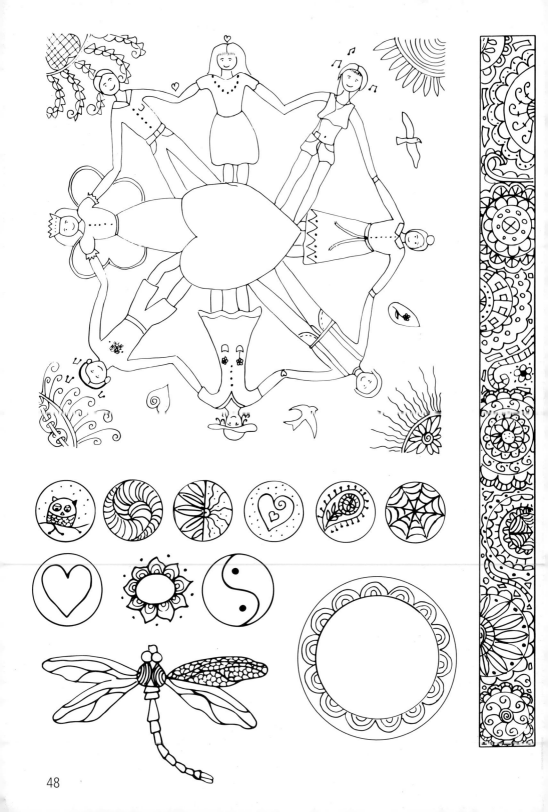